W9-AWJ-562

Willie Shoemaker

By
Louis Phillips

Edited By
Michael E. Goodman

CRESTWOOD HOUSE

Mankato, Minnesota
U.S.A.

Phillips, Louis.
   Willie Shoemaker.

(SCU-2)
   SUMMARY: Presents a biography of the jockey nicknamed "The Shoe" who won his fourth Kentucky Derby at the age of fifty-four.
   1. Shoemaker, Willie—Juvenile literature. 2. Jockeys—United States—Biography—Juvenile literature.
[1. Shoemaker, Willie. 2. Jockeys] I. Goodman, Michael E. II. Title. III. Series.
SF336.S47P47   1988   798.4′3′0924   [B]   [92]   88-14966
ISBN 0-89686-381-6

International Standard	Library of Congress
Book Number:	Catalog Card Number:
0-89686-381-6	88-14966

PHOTO CREDITS

Cover: Focus West
Focus West: 8-9, 10-11, 16, 21, 25, 32-33, 38-39; (S. Stidham) 4, 15, 22, 27, 36, 40-41, 43, 44-45; (Diane Johnson) 12, 18-19; (Rick Stewart) 30
Wide World Photos: 7, 42, 47

Produced by Carnival Enterprises.

CRESTWOOD HOUSE

TABLE OF CONTENTS

And They're Off 5

An Outstanding Athlete 10

Shoe in a Shoe Box 13

"I Wanted to be a Rider" 17

First Victory and Beyond 22

A New World Record 26

First Victory at Kentucky 28

One of the Greatest Mistakes in Sports History 29

"Mostly My Career Has Always Gone Up" 31

Records Gained and Missed 34

A Major Accident 36

There's No Reason To Stop 40

Willie Shoemaker's Professional Statistics . . . 48

AND THEY'RE OFF!

It was a sunny May day in 1986. A crowd of 123,819 horse racing fans had gathered at Churchill Downs in Louisville, Kentucky. Millions more had gathered in front of their television sets to watch the 112th running of the Kentucky Derby.

The Kentucky Derby is to horse racing what the World Series is to baseball. To win the Derby is to win racing's highest honor. Just to ride in the Derby is a dream come true for any jockey.

Willie Shoemaker had already ridden in 23 Kentucky Derby races, more than any other jockey, and had won that great race three times. His fourth win would come on this day. "The Shoe," at age 54, was to become the oldest Derby winner ever. And what a victory it was!

On that day, Willie was riding a horse named Ferdinand. But very few people thought Ferdinand had much of a chance of winning. For one thing, Willie was an older jockey who would be racing against jockeys half his age. Would he be strong and clever enough? Would his reflexes be quick enough? Most of the experts and fans thought that a horse named Snow Chief would win the race and wear the wreath of roses given to the winner.

The weather for the Derby was perfect. Before going out onto the track, Charlie Whittingham—the man who trained Ferdinand—gave his jockey some final instructions. He told Willie, "Get position and do the best you can." He meant that Willie should make sure that

Willie Shoemaker has ridden in more than 37,000 horse races.

Ferdinand wasn't blocked out by the other horses.

The horses entered the starting gate and they waited for the signal to start the mile-and-a-quarter "run for the roses."

The bugle sounded. "They're off!" shouted the track announcer.

The horses broke from the gate. Snow Chief and other horses raced ahead so quickly that Ferdinand could not find an opening. He had to drop back while the other horses raced free.

After a quarter mile, Ferdinand was in ninth position. After half a mile, Ferdinand was in 16th place—dead last! Groovy and Snow Chief were burning up the track, running the first half-mile in 45½ seconds. It did not look as if Willie Shoemaker and Ferdinand would have a chance.

"I wasn't in any hurry to rush up quickly," Willie said later. "I thought, 'I'll just take my time and gradually pick up the field and try to save as much ground as I can.'"

Ferdinand started to gain ground and pass other horses. As the horses reached the top of the stretch (that part of the track where the horses run as fast as they can straight toward the finish line), Ferdinand was in fifth place. The horses ahead of him appeared to be a solid wall. Willie had about three seconds to make up his mind: should he go to the outside and avoid the other horses, or should he try to dart between the horses and get ahead of the pack?

At last, there was a narrow opening inside, near the rail. Willie pushed Ferdinand between two horses, and Ferdinand started to pull away. He crossed the finish line

The winner and his wreath of roses!

The Shoe knows just how to move his horse into the first-place position.

more than two lengths ahead of runner-up Bold Arrangement (in horse racing, a "length" refers to the length of a race horse, from its nose to its tail). All 123,189 fans were on their feet, screaming, shouting, jumping up and down.

The Shoe had done it!

Ferdinand's owner, Howard B. Keck, was joyous. He told reporters, "I think Willie made an excellent move. It may

have been the race right there. He made a move on the backstretch, and then he made a move at the head of the stretch. He rides most of our horses, and we've won our share."

When Ferdinand was led into the Winner's Circle to receive his wreath of roses, Willie had tears in his eyes. The grand old man of racing had shown the younger jockeys a thing or two.

Jockeys need strength in their arms and legs to control a racing thoroughbred.

AN OUTSTANDING ATHLETE

There is something very exciting about watching well-trained horses thundering down a track. The horses gallop with grace and speed and are guided by some of the finest

athletes in the world. Very few people realize how difficult
it is to be a jockey. Although they are small and light,
jockeys require great strength in their hands and legs to
control a galloping thoroughbred weighing over a thousand
pounds. They must have good judgment, a great sense of
timing, careful balance, and above all, courage. As the

11

horse gallops at top speed, a jockey must guide it to the finish line as other horses gallop close on either side.

Of the thousands and thousands of jockeys who have ever raced, Willie Shoemaker may well be the best. During his career, he has ridden more winners than any other jockey. He has become a legend.

Willie Shoemaker has ridden in more than 37,000 races and has won 8,500 times. He has come in second 5,700 times. And he has finished third 4,600 times. The horses that he has ridden have earned more than $100,000,000. Willie Shoemaker has won the Kentucky Derby four times, and has won another very important horse race, The Belmont Stakes, five times.

As fellow jockey Eddie Arcaro has stated, "Regardless of the particular sport, Willie Shoemaker, by his accomplishments, must be considered one of the outstanding athletes in the history of sports."

SHOE IN A SHOE BOX

Willie Shoemaker's nickname is "The Shoe." A nickname based on an athlete's name is not at all unusual. What is amazing, however, is that a shoe box once helped save Willie's life!

William Lee Shoemaker was born in Fabens, Texas, on August 19, 1931. At birth, Willie weighed only 2½ pounds. The doctor who delivered Willie shook his head and sadly told Willie's mother that the tiny baby would not live

Before a race, Willie exercises his horse.

through the night.

Willie's grandmother, however, refused to believe the doctor. She was determined to save her grandson's life. She took Willie Lee and placed the baby inside a shoe box. To stop him from shivering, she opened the stove, warmed the oven, and placed Willie and his box inside. She carefully watched over the tiny baby through the night. The next morning Willie was still alive! The child's fragile life had been saved.

Throughout his life, Willie Lee had some major obstacles to overcome. He was born during the Depression, a time when jobs and money were hard to find. His family had to move from town to town in order to find work.

Willie Lee was very small and lightweight. He was always the smallest boy in his classes at school. He had to prove his abilities against boys who were much taller and who weighed much more than he did. When Willie Lee went to high school in El Monte, California, he weighed only 80 pounds, but he was determined to prove himself. He joined the boxing and wrestling teams, and was never defeated in competition!

When Willie Lee was a freshman in high school, a girl in his class named Joyce was dating a jockey. She noticed Willie's build and suggested that he ride horses for a living. At the time, Willie didn't know anything about horse racing, but he decided to follow his friend's advice. Joyce's boyfriend took Willie to a horse ranch and introduced Willie to the owners. At age 16, Willie started his first job.

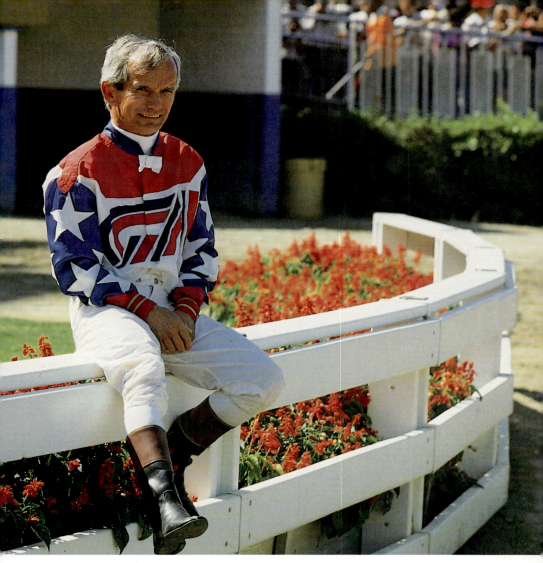

Willie Shoemaker began his racing career when he was 18 years old.

He was soon earning $75 a month, working as a stableboy at the Suzy Q. Ranch in Phente, California.

At the end of a race, The Shoe stands up in the saddle to slow down his horse.

16

"I WANTED TO BE A RIDER"

Working on a ranch was difficult. The hours were long and the chores were tough. The stables had to be swept daily, and the horses had to be exercised, washed, combed, brushed, and fed. As soon as he had finished one chore, Willie started another one. At night he slept in the stables curled up on the straw.

But no matter how hard the work was, Willie kept his mind on his goal. He was determined to become a jockey — not just any jockey, but the best jockey. Thinking back on that time, Willie wrote, "Right from the word go, I wanted to be a rider. I knew I had to work hard to impress on people that I was serious about what I wanted to be. I figured if I worked hard and showed an interest, they would show an interest in me."

So Willie worked hard. He practiced and learned. Horse racing is a very difficult sport to master. A jockey must have very strong hands, arms, shoulders, and legs. He must know how to become a true partner with his horse. He needs to know how to "talk" to his horse — how to make a timid horse brave or how to quiet a high-strung horse. In addition to physical strength, a good jockey needs mental quickness. He must make decisions very quickly — when to hold a horse back or when to cut to the outside, go to the rail, or take advantage of an opening between horses running in front of him.

In addition, becoming a jockey involves a big investment. Jockeys must buy all of their own equipment, except for "the silks" (the riding cap and shirt). The silks are supplied by the owner of the horse. Everything else,

The colorful silks of the rider are provided by the owner of the horse.

including riding pants, boots, whip, spurs, saddle, and saddle cloth (items called "the tack"), jockeys must buy for themselves.

Willie had a lot to learn about the sport and business of

racing, but he kept at it. Soon a man named George Reeves gave Willie a chance to become a jockey. Reeves had watched Willie exercising horses at the Santa Anita race track. On April 20, 1949, when Willie was 18 years old, Reeves told Willie he was going to ride in his first race. Willie was given a horse named Waxahachie to ride. He didn't win that first race; he finished fifth. But he was lucky to finish the race at all!

During a race, jockeys usually wear two pairs of goggles because of flying dust and dirt on the track. When one pair becomes too covered with mud or dirt to see through, the jockey pulls that first pair down his neck and then pulls the second pair over his eyes. In his first race, Willie wore only one pair of goggles. Soon he couldn't see where he was going. Luckily, Waxahachie knew where she was going, so horse and rider managed to finish the race without an accident. But finishing fifth is not the same as finishing first. No one knew that better than Willie.

Willie didn't win his second race, either. He knew he needed to work harder. He needed to concentrate more. He watched the other jockeys and studied how they sat and how they used their hands.

It was his third race that started him on the road to winning.

Because of a track's dust and dirt, jockeys wear two pairs of goggles when racing.

A good jockey must be able to "talk" to his horse.

FIRST VICTORY AND BEYOND

April 20, 1949, is a special date in Willie Shoemaker's life. That was when he won his very first race. At Golden Gate Fields in California, trainer George Reeves gave Willie a horse named Shafter V to ride. Willie brought

Shafter V across the finish line first. It was an exciting moment for an apprentice, or first-year jockey.

After that first taste of victory, Willie rode faster and better. Before the end of 1949, he had ridden 219 winners—in less than nine months! Only one other jockey in the country won more races that year. Willie was quickly gaining the respect of the horse owners, trainers, and fellow jockeys. Horse racing fans began to notice Willie and to cheer for the young man they called "The Shoe."

One great jockey who took interest in Willie was Eddie Arcaro. For more than 30 years, Arcaro had been one of the world's greatest jockeys. He noticed that Willie had good touch, balance, and strength. He was also impressed with the strength of Willie's hands. Arcaro decided to help Willie improve his riding style.

"I learned a lot from Eddie," Willie said later in his career. "I watched how he brought a horse out of the gate, how he sat, how he whipped. It helped me."

The two jockeys became great friends. Arcaro not only helped Willie improve his horse racing skills, he also taught him how to get along better with sportswriters and the public. The writers were calling Willie "Silent Shoe" because he was so quiet. With Arcaro's help, Willie learned how to be comfortable around other people. He also learned to answer each writers' question and how to explain his feelings about life and racing.

Willie was the second-best jockey of 1949, but in 1950, he was number one. He rode 388 winners. No jockey rode more winners that year, and only jockey Joe Culmone rode as many. Shoe and Culmone tied a 44-year-old record for the most winners ridden in a single year.

Willie won so many races that often a horse was made a favorite to win a race just because Shoe was riding him. Fans at the Del Mar race track in California joked that the race track should change its name from Del Mar to Shoemaker Downs.

It seemed that nothing could stop Willie. One day while he was at the beach, he stepped on a stingray. The poison from the stingray caused Willie's foot to swell so badly that he couldn't wear his riding boot. One of the track assistants took a knife, slit a hole in the boot, and got it on Willie's foot. In spite of the swelling and the pain, Shoe won four races that day!

Soon Willie began looking for new challenges. He had proved his skills to the fans on the West Coast. Now he wanted to show the people in the East what he could do. In 1951, when The Shoe was 20 years old, he went to New York City for the first time. On the very first day that he rode in front of New York racing fans, The Shoe brought home three winners. One of his winners earned $50,000 — and Shoe received ten percent of the winnings. In 1950, Shoe's horses won prizes of $844,040. Not only was The Shoe becoming a skilled jockey, he was on his way to becoming a very rich man as well.

The Shoe is considered one of the greatest jockeys in horse racing history.

A NEW WORLD RECORD

Willie once told a reporter that records never really meant much to him. "Sure," he said, "when you get close to one, it's nice to go on and break it, but I've never set any records as a goal—they just happened. When they come, they come. Records are made and records are broken all the time. All of them will be broken, eventually, including all of mine."

The first major record that "just happened" to Willie occurred in October 1953. On that day he rode his 392nd winner to set the world record for most victories by a jockey in one calendar year. By the end of the year he added to that record. He finished with a grand total of 485 wins!

But there were more worlds to conquer. Just as every baseball player dreams of playing in the World Series, and just as every football player wants to take part in the Super Bowl, every jockey wants to win the Kentucky Derby in Louisville, Kentucky.

The Derby is a one-and-a-quarter mile long race that tests a horse's speed and strength. It also tests a jockey's skill.

Willie had ridden in the Kentucky Derby in 1952, 1953, and 1954, but had never won. It was not until 1955, when the eyes of the racing world were on the two finest horses in the world, Nashua and Swaps, that Willie showed everybody he was indeed the best.

A racing thoroughbred can sometimes be a hard animal to control.

FIRST VICTORY AT KENTUCKY

Willie Shoemaker has said that for him nothing is more enjoyable than being on a horse—especially, he jokes, "on a horse that wants to get across the finish line first."

Shoe must have found riding Swaps a very enjoyable experience indeed. Few thoroughbreds have ever wanted to get across the finish line first so much. In 1955, Willie was given the honor to ride the great horse Swaps in the Kentucky Derby. But as great a horse as Swaps was, he was not the horse favored to win the race. The favorite horse was Nashua, and Nashua was being ridden by Shoe's great friend and rival, Eddie Arcaro. Sportswriters and fans felt that Arcaro would guide Nashua across the finish line first. Some others even thought Summer Tan was the horse to beat.

From the time the horses broke from the starting gate, the spectators knew that it was going to be a fast and close race. The horses made the far turn and started down the stretch to the finish line. Swaps was in the lead, but only by a neck. Shoe started to cluck in Swap's ear (jockeys frequently cluck into their horses' ears to make them run faster) and urged the horse to pour on the speed. Swaps pulled away from Nashua and opened up a lead of one length. When Swaps crossed the finish line first, a great cheer went up from the crowd. Shoe had done it! Even at the finish, Swaps was still pulling away from the other horses. He set a new world record for a one-and-a-quarter mile race. Shoe had scored his first Derby victory. How sweet it was!

ONE OF THE GREATEST MISTAKES IN SPORTS HISTORY

After winning the Kentucky Derby in 1955, and after becoming the first American jockey to win purses totaling more than $2,000,000 in 1956, Willie Shoemaker was on top of the world. But he took a big fall the next year. At the 1957 Kentucky Derby, Shoe committed one of the worst mistakes in horse racing history. Willie has never forgotten that mistake.

In the 1957 Derby, Shoe chose to ride a horse named Gallant Man, owned by a man named Lowe. In his autobiography, Shoe wrote that on the night before the Derby, Mr. Lowe told him a dream about a jockey riding his horse and misjudging where the finish line was. Shoe said, "Oh, Mr. Lowe, don't worry about that. I've ridden in this race too many times. It's not going to happen."

Unfortunately, that is exactly what did happen. Gallant Man's owner had a dream that came true!

Riding Gallant Man toward the finish line, Willie found himself fighting for the lead with a horse named Iron Liege ridden by Bill Hartack. Gallant Man took the lead, but then

Willie, thinking that the 16th pole was actually the finish line, stood up in the stirrups (race tracks are marked by long poles to help jockeys judge the distance of each race). Willie was 1/16th of a mile off! At that moment, Iron Liege nosed past Shoe's horse and won.

No one could believe what they had seen — not the fans, the other jockeys, or the race track officials. The great Willie Shoemaker had made a terrible mistake, a mistake that cost his horse a Kentucky Derby win. The stewards (the officials who oversee the running of the race), after viewing films of the race and talking to Willie, had no choice. They suspended Willie from racing for 15 days for "gross carelessness."

Cheers had turned to boos. It had been a fast trip from the top to the bottom.

"MOSTLY MY CAREER HAS ALWAYS GONE UP"

After the Kentucky Derby defeat, Shoe felt depressed, but he refused to allow his life to be ruled by a mistake. Later he said, "I thought I couldn't do anything wrong. As it turned out, that experience really did help me."

All great athletes learn from their mistakes, and Shoe was no exception. He turned his attention to future races. The mistake in Kentucky was a low point, but it passed. In 1958 his spirits picked up considerably when he achieved

Willie Shoemaker has always been serious about riding horses.

Even after his racing mistake at the Kentucky Derby, The Shoe
continued to ride horses and win races.

his 3,000th victory.

Then in 1959 he was elected to the Jockey's Hall of Fame. In May of that year, Shoe redeemed himself in Kentucky when he won his second Derby.

In that Derby, Shoe rode a horse named Tomy Lee. A horse named Sword Dancer took the lead on the final turn, and it appeared that Tomy Lee would finish a close second. In the final 200 yards of the race, the horses ran neck and neck. A length from the the finish line, Sword Dancer still held the narrowest of leads. But Shoe, using every bit of strength in his powerful hands, almost lifted Tomy Lee's head across the finish line first. In the closest race in the history of the Kentucky Derby, Tomy Lee won by the tip of his nose!

Willie was a hero once again. Everyone from stableboy to horse owner cheered for Shoe and his extraordinary talent.

Greg Knight, a well-known horse trainer, said of Shoe, "Shoe's not a wrestler. His strength is his coolness on a horse." But perhaps the highest compliment of all came from a fellow jockey who told a reporter, "All of us talk to horses, but with Shoe it seems like they talk back."

RECORDS GAINED AND MISSED

Jockeys are lucky in one respect. Their careers usually are longer than the careers of baseball or football players.

And The Shoe was no exception—he just got better and better.

Up until May of 1961, only jockeys Eddie Arcaro and Johnny Longden had ever ridden home more than 4,000 winners. But on May 19, 1961, aboard a horse named Guaranteeya, Willie Shoemaker joined that select company. Now there was no doubt—Willie was one of the best jockeys ever. Three years later, he won his 5,000th race. At that time only Johnny Longden had more victories.

Still, with every career there are high points and low points. No matter how many records The Shoe was able to achieve, there was one record that kept eluding him—The Triple Crown.

In baseball, a hitter gets the Triple Crown if he leads his league in batting average, home runs, and runs-batted-in during a single season. Horse racing has its Triple Crown, too. If a horse and/or jockey wins the Kentucky Derby, the Preakness, and the Belmont Stakes in a single season, he or she is said to have won the Triple Crown of racing. The Shoe, of course, has won all those races (the Kentucky Derby four times, the Preakness twice, and the Belmont Stakes five times) but he has never won them all in a single season. He has never won the Triple Crown. But he has never stopped trying, either.

Shoe won many races between 1964 and 1968, including the 1965 Kentucky Derby. But then disaster struck. During a race in early 1968, Shoe nearly lost his life and his career.

Jockeys use their leg muscles to ride a few inches above the saddle.

A MAJOR ACCIDENT

Not only was The Shoe an immensely talented jockey, he

was also a very lucky one. For nearly two decades of hard riding, he had escaped the serious injuries that frequently bother other athletes. But on January 23, 1968, while riding in a race at Santa Anita, The Shoe took a terrible spill.

In that race, Shoe was riding directly behind an apprentice jockey named Juan Gonzalez. Gonzalez was aboard a horse named Kodiak Kid. Kodiak Kid stumbled and fell. The Shoe was too close to turn his own horse out of the way, and he went down. As he lay on the track, the other jockeys galloped by, narrowly missing him. "I just couldn't get up," Shoe recalled.

He was rushed to the hospital. Doctors told Willie he had broken the femur bone in his right leg and would not be able to ride for at least the rest of the year. But Willie was frightened. Would he be able to ride again? The question haunted Willie. For the first time in his life, he began to worry about his ability. But, with encouragement from his family and friends, Shoe didn't give up. He was determined to ride again. He exercised, he trained. Finally, he and his doctors agreed on the day for his attempted comeback. Could he do it?

On February 11, 1969, nearly 13 months after his accident, Willie climbed aboard a filly (a female horse) named Princess Endeavor. He rode her across the finish line first. It was his comeback race, and he came home a winner! But more than winning, he had proved he could go on racing.

" . . . and they're off!"

The Shoe (No. 7) pulls into the lead.

THERE'S NO REASON TO STOP

For nearly 20 years after his near-fatal accident at Santa Anita, Shoe has gone on riding. He has set record after record. First 6,000 victories. Then 7,000. Then the unheard

of 8,000 victories. No wonder when racing fans discuss who is the greatest jockey of all time, Willie Shoemaker's name often heads the list. It is one thing for a jockey to have one great season. It is quite another for a jockey to go on compiling great season after great season for nearly four decades!

Willie and his wife Cindy celebrate after another victory.

The Shoe poses with children representing the Muscular Dystrophy Association.

Today, Shoe lives with his wife Cindy and two children in California. When he is not racing, he is very active as a fund-raiser for charities. He has been especially active in raising money for the Hemophilia Foundation. He owns a ranch in Arizona, and has invested his money in gas stations, oil wells, and restaurants. He has many interests,

Sometimes a horse was named the favorite to win because The Shoe was riding it—and he usually did win!

but racing still holds his heart. And he keeps on winning.

In 1985, at the age of 54, Willie became the first jockey in history whose horses surpassed $100,000,000 in career earnings. Today he is the oldest active jockey in the United States. In spite of his age, he rides the way he did when he

was 20 years younger. "I guess the only thing different about the way I ride now compared to a few years ago," he has said, "is that I don't get as low in the saddle" — jockeys use their powerful leg muscles to sit only a few inches above the saddle.

In 1986 Willie astounded the sports world when he won, the Kentucky Derby for the fourth time! One year later, he again triumphed at one of the most important races in America, the Breeders' Cup. Riding a horse named Ferdinand (the same horse he had ridden to the Kentucky Derby win), Shoe won the $3,000,000 race, beating out another Kentucky Derby winner, Alysheba. It was a stretch drive between two great horses, and Ferdinand won by a nose!

Willie Shoemaker is a king in the Sport of Kings. As he has said on more than one occasion, "I'm not hungry anymore. I've made enough money. But I love what I do. As long as I do it well, there's no reason to stop."

In 1987, Willie Shoemaker was the oldest active jockey in the United States.

WILLIE SHOEMAKER'S PROFESSIONAL STATISTICS

1949 Wins his first horse race

1950 Ties a record by riding 388 winners in a single year

1953 Sets a record by riding 485 winners in a single year

1955 Wins the Kentucky Derby

1957 Wins the Belmont Stakes

1959 Elected to the Jockey's Hall of Fame; wins the Kentucky Derby and the Belmont Stakes

1961 Achieves his 4,000th victory

1962 Wins six races on a single racing program; wins the Belmont Stakes

1963 Wins the Preakness

1964 Achieves his 5,000th victory

1965 Wins the Kentucky Derby

1967 Wins the Preakness and the Belmont Stakes

1970 Achieves his 6,000th victory

1975 Wins the Belmont Stakes

1976 Achieves his 7,000th victory

1981 Achieves his 8,000th victory; elected to the National Museum of Racing Hall of Fame

1986 Achieves his 8,500th victory; wins the Kentucky Derby

1987 Wins the Breeders' Cup

DATE DUE			

B
SHO   Phillips, Louis.   **15370**

Willie Shoemaker.

NEWPORT ELEMENTARY LIBRARY

850407 01281   13526B